THE ANIMAL CELL AND DIVISION BIOLOGY FOR KIDS

CHILDREN'S BIOLOGY BOOKS

BABY PROFESSOR

EDUCATION KIDS

Let's talk about the structure of life and its divisions. Each living thing on Earth is composed of trillions of cells. Cells are the basic structures of life. Animals and plants are formed when cells are joined together.

Animals are also composed
of trillions of cells, like
all other living things. In
this book, you will learn
amazing facts about the
animal cell and the cell
division.

ANIMAL CELL

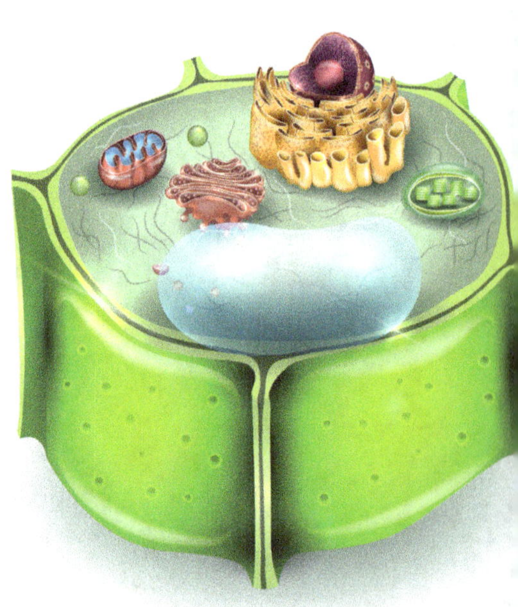

PLANT CELL

WHAT IS THE DIFFERENCE BETWEEN THE ANIMAL CELL AND THE PLANT CELL?

The plant cell makes the plants independent because it can make its own food while an animal cell is incapable of making its own food.

Nonetheless, an animal cell is considered self-sufficient because it can produce everything it needs. This means that an animal cell is capable of making its own components or structures.

This is because animal cells are composed of nano-chemical factories. An example of this is the Golgi complex which can generate what it needs. It produces its own components.

Each cell in the animal body has its amazing function depending on its type. Animal cells are composed of the main parts, namely: the nucleus, the cell membrane, and the cytoplasm.

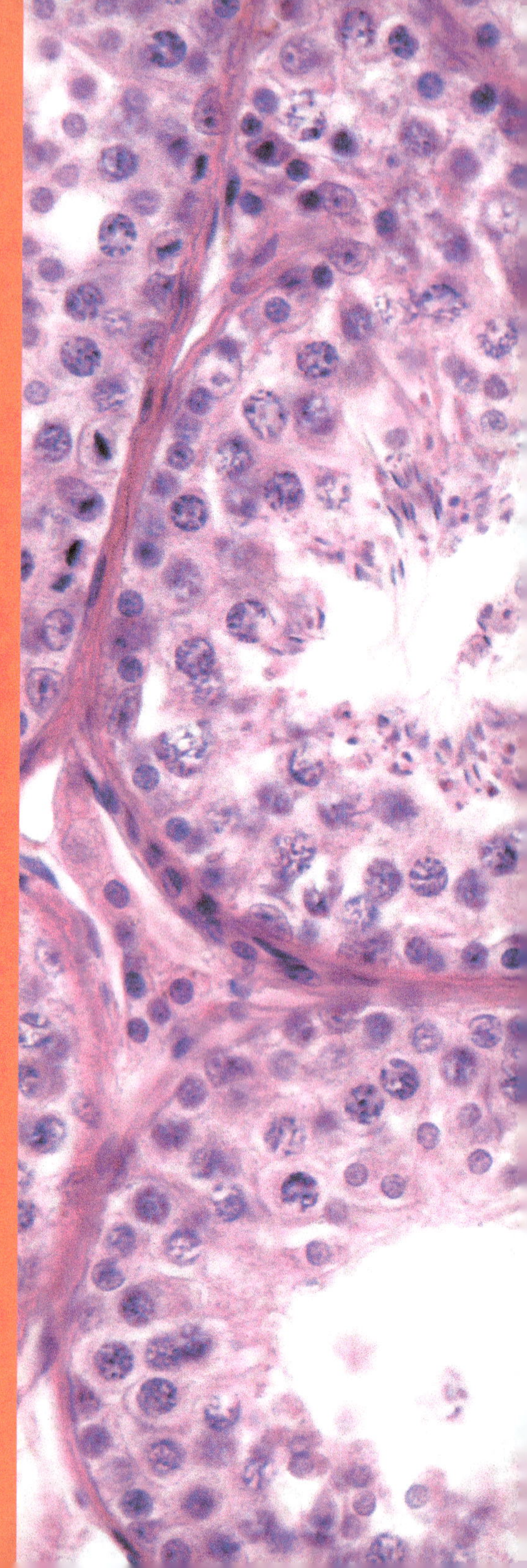

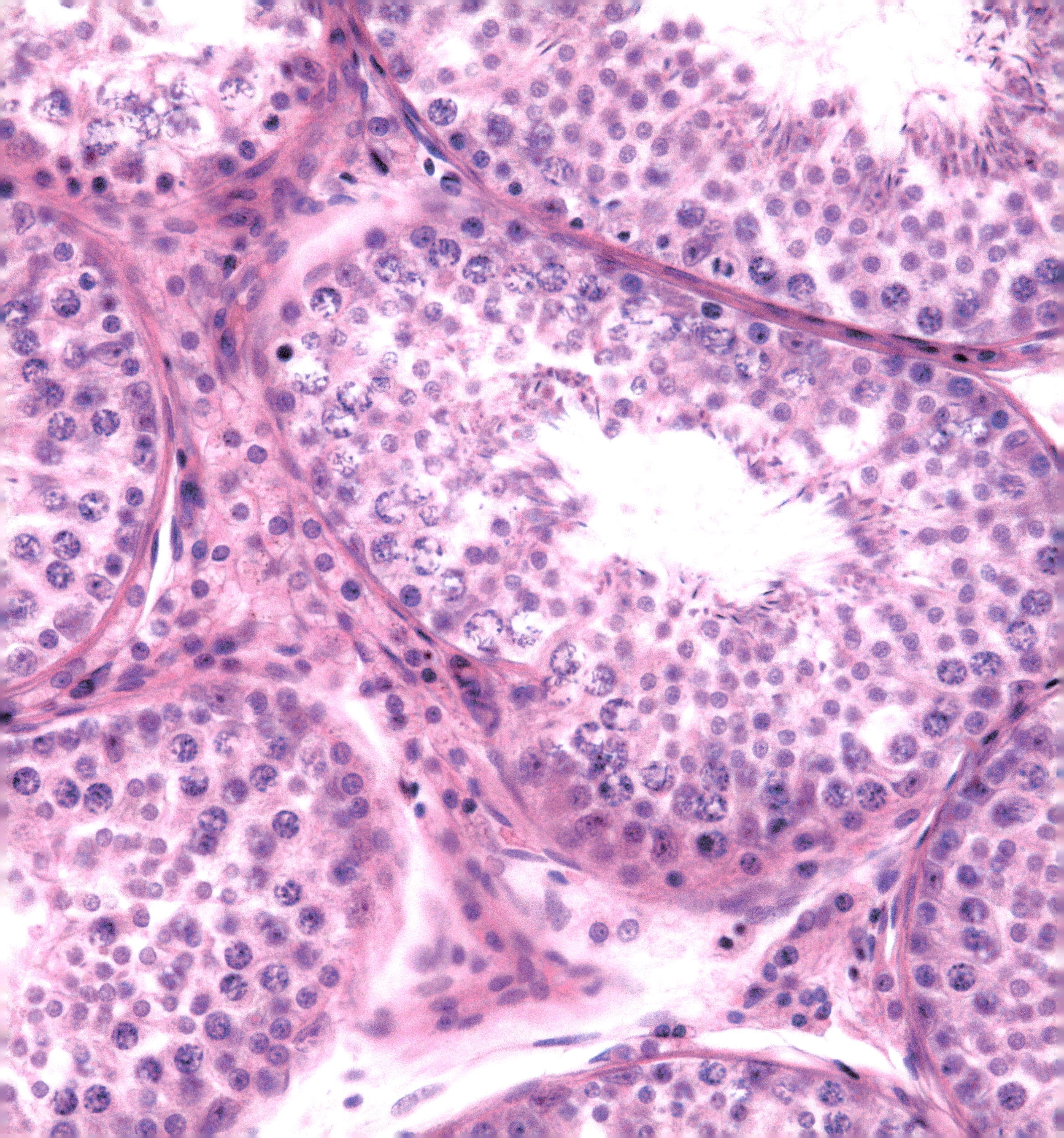

Nucleus

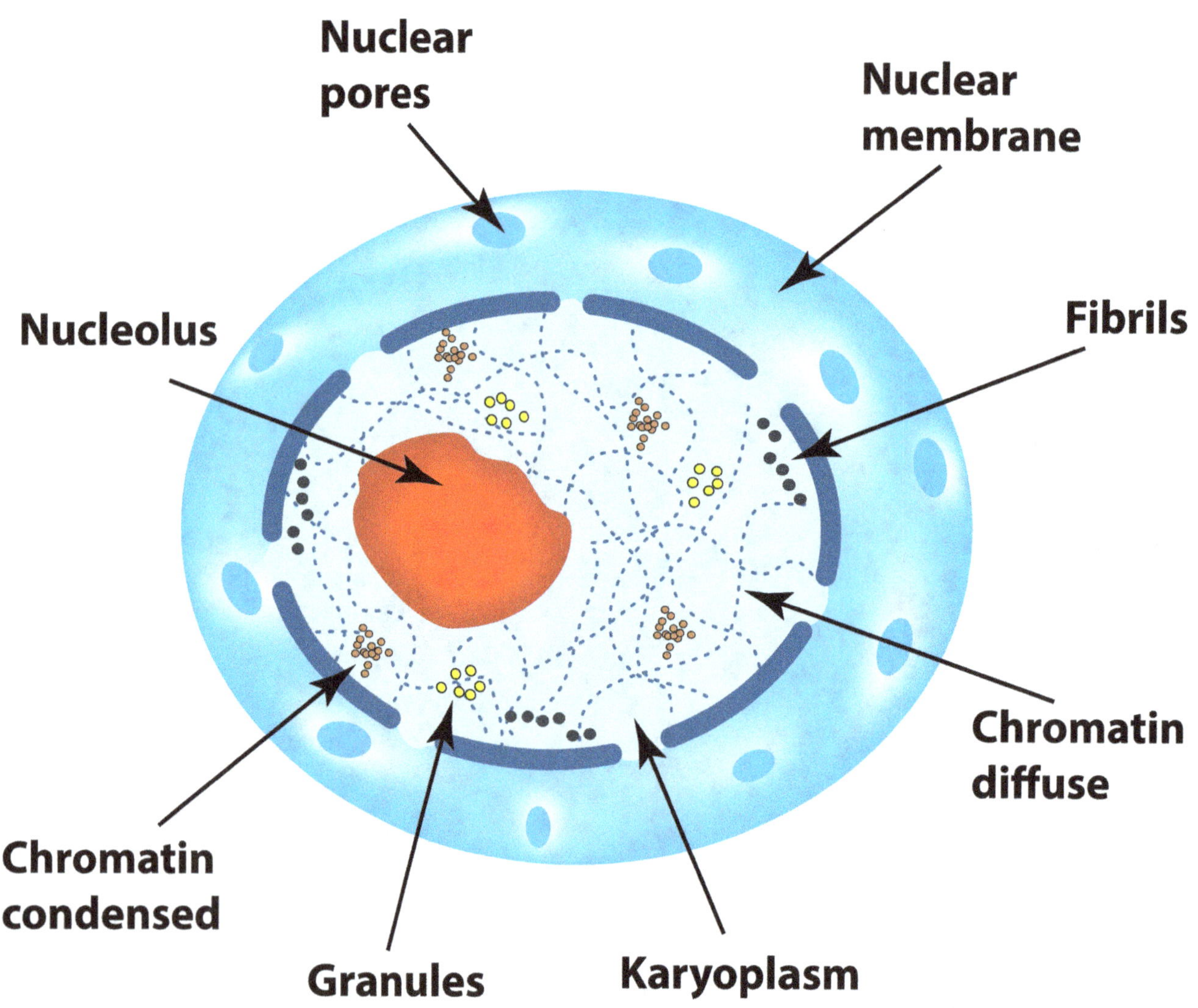

Nuclear pores
Nuclear membrane
Nucleolus
Fibrils
Chromatin condensed
Chromatin diffuse
Granules
Karyoplasm

NUCLEUS

The Nucleus is the brain of the cell. The nucleus is responsible for guiding and giving directions to the cell as to what it will do.

Without the nucleus, the cell could not function. In fact, the nucleus has the capability of making the needed cell organelles. The nucleus is located anywhere in the cell.

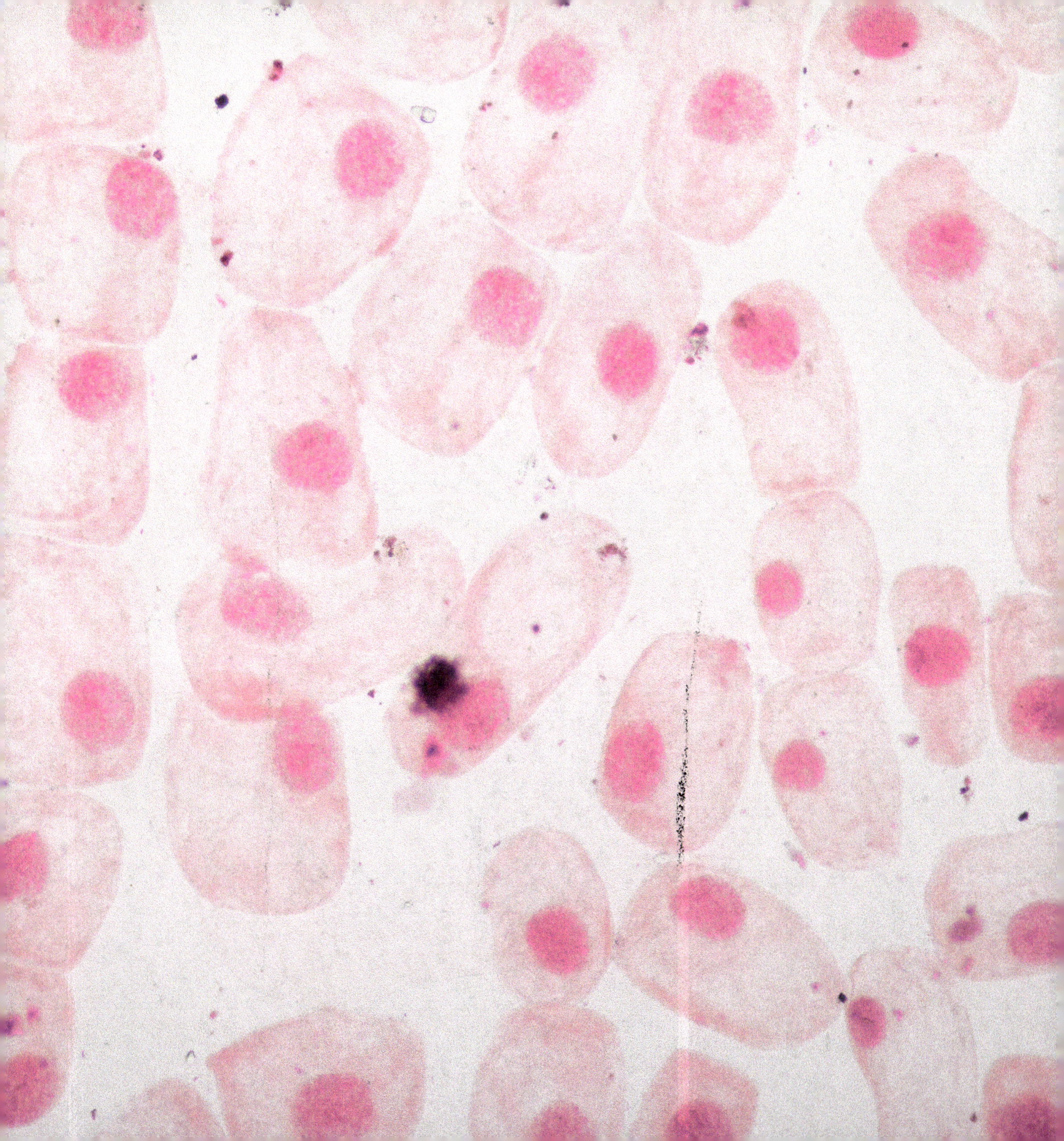

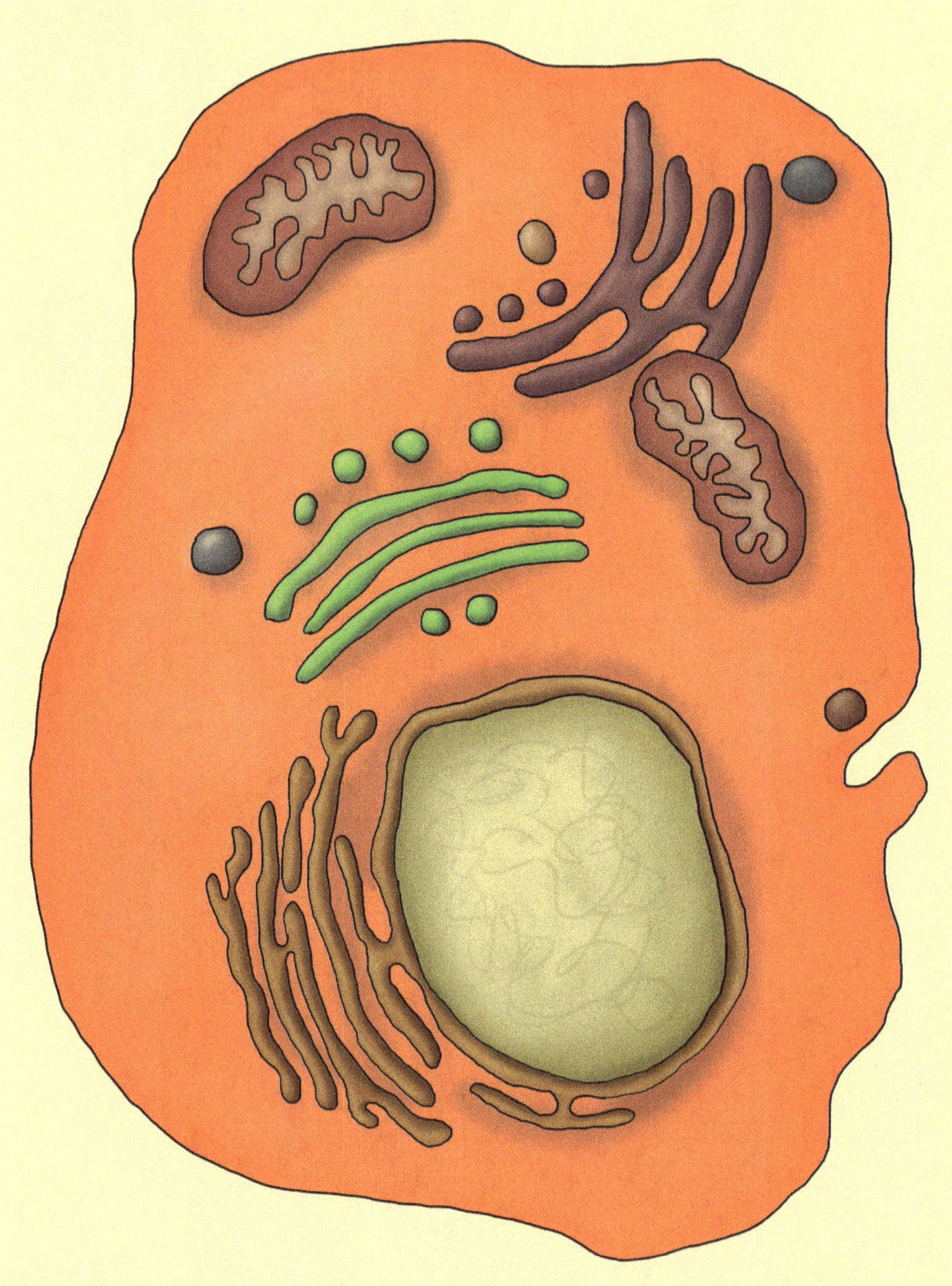

However, it is important to know that only the eukaryotic cells have a nucleus. The nucleus is an organelle that stores the cell's genetic information in the form of DNA or deoxyribonucleic acid.

CELL MEMBRANE

The cell membrane protects the animal cells. It serves as the best guard of the cell. It protects the cell from harmful objects.

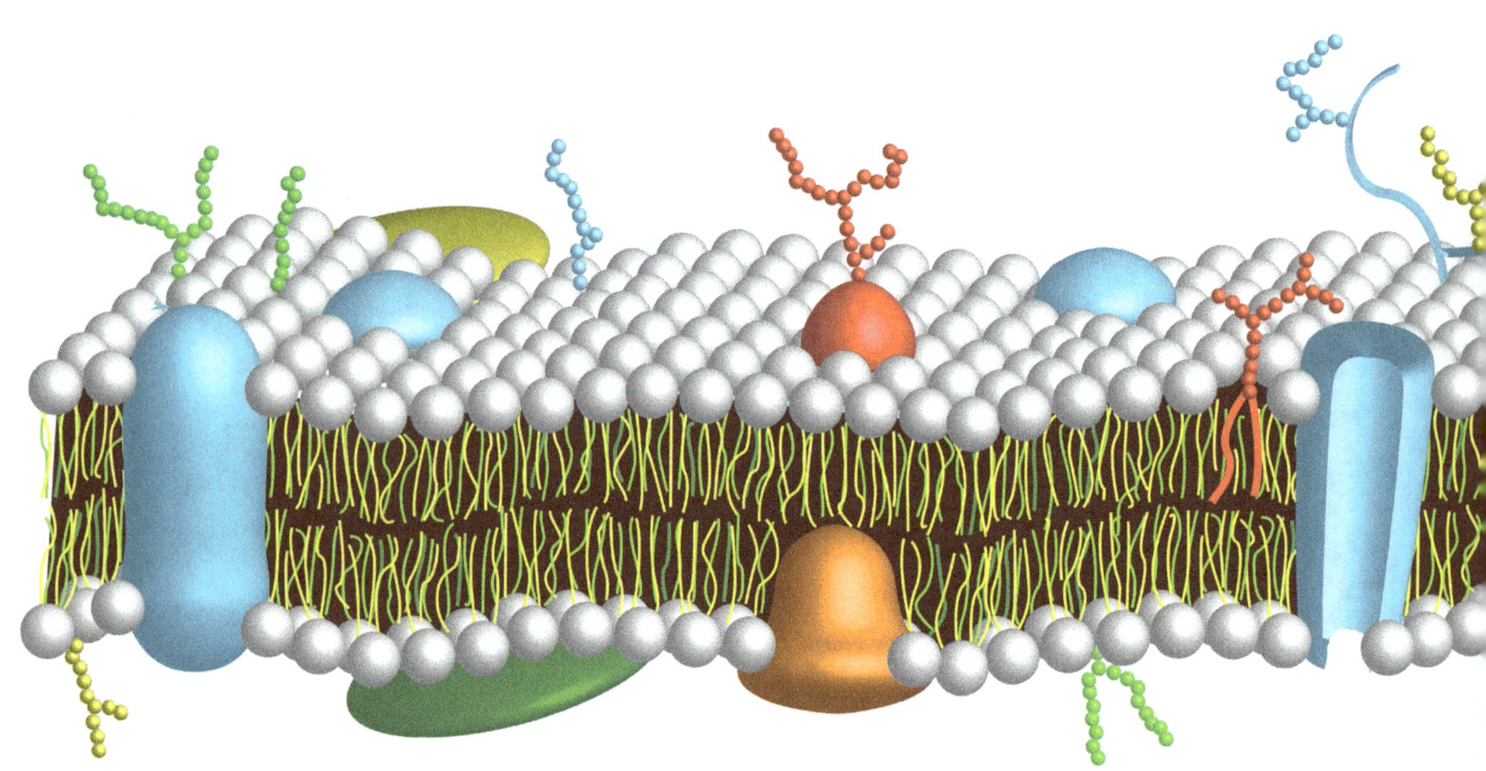

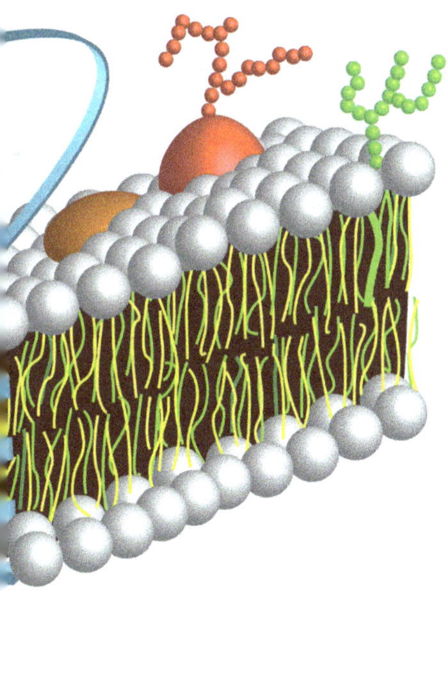

CYTOPLASM

The cytoplasm is responsible for giving shape to the cell. It is the component of the cell that keeps organelles in their places.

It is made of protein. The cytoplasm makes sure the function of the organelles to transport materials is done properly.

The cytoplasm also helps in breaking down the wastes of the cells. Inside the cytoplasm is a cytoskeleton. Just like the plant cells, animal cells are eukaryotic cells but they are very different in their structures.

A plant cell is bigger than an animal cell. An animal cell comes in diverse sizes and has an irregular shape.

Plant cell

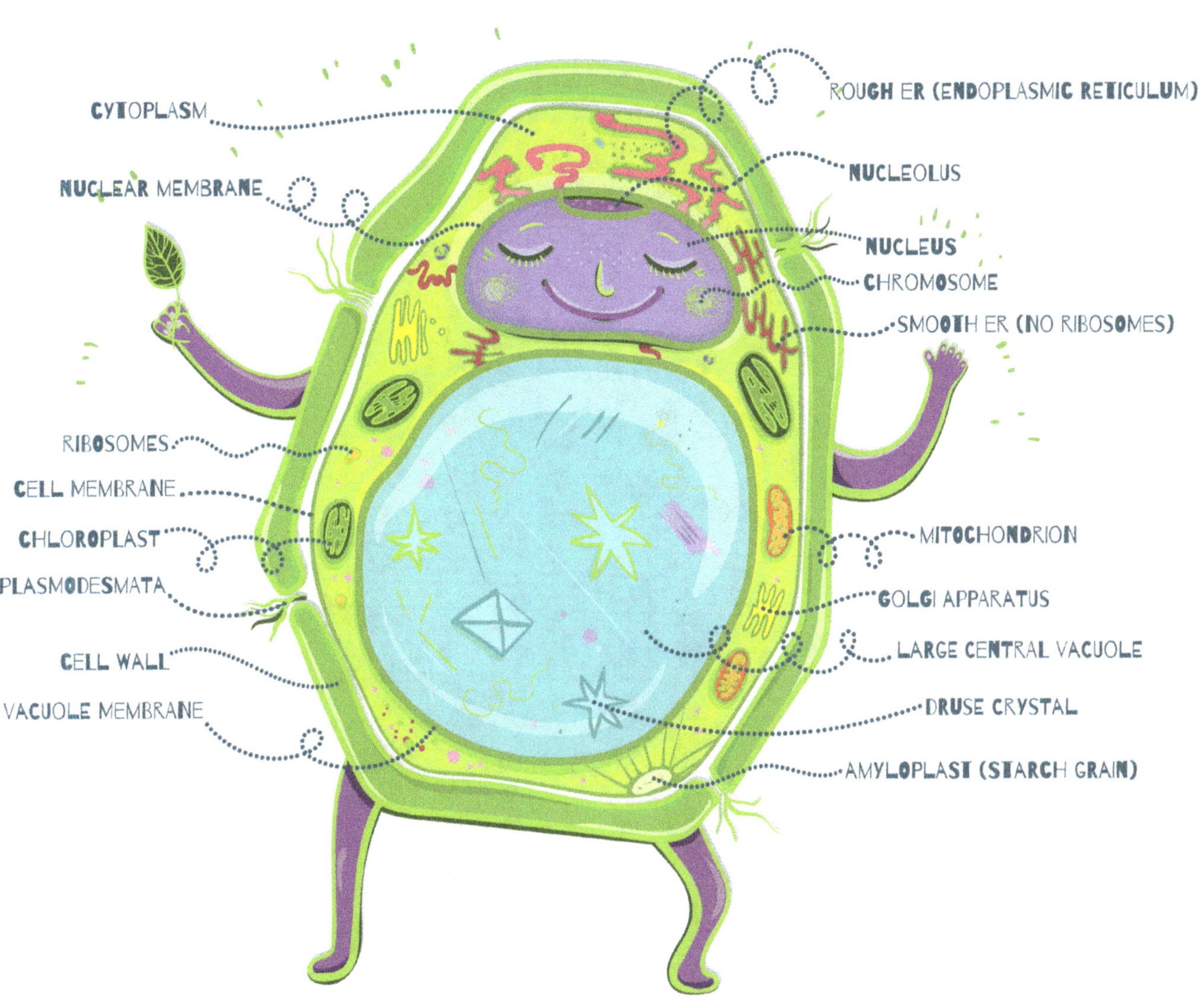

CYTOPLASM
NUCLEAR MEMBRANE
RIBOSOMES
CELL MEMBRANE
CHLOROPLAST
PLASMODESMATA
CELL WALL
VACUOLE MEMBRANE
ROUGH ER (ENDOPLASMIC RETICULUM)
NUCLEOLUS
NUCLEUS
CHROMOSOME
SMOOTH ER (NO RIBOSOMES)
MITOCHONDRION
GOLGI APPARATUS
LARGE CENTRAL VACUOLE
DRUSE CRYSTAL
AMYLOPLAST (STARCH GRAIN)

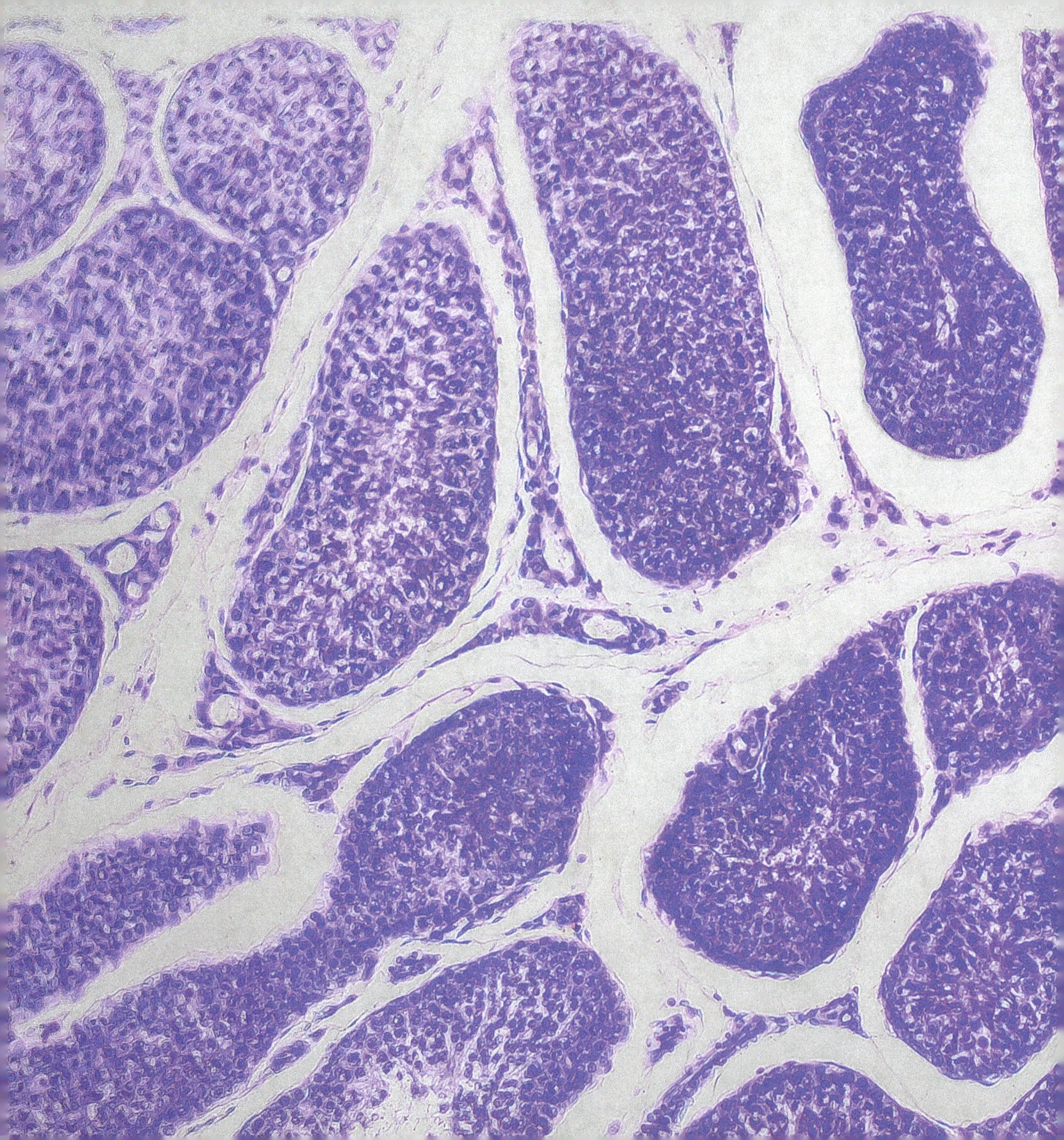

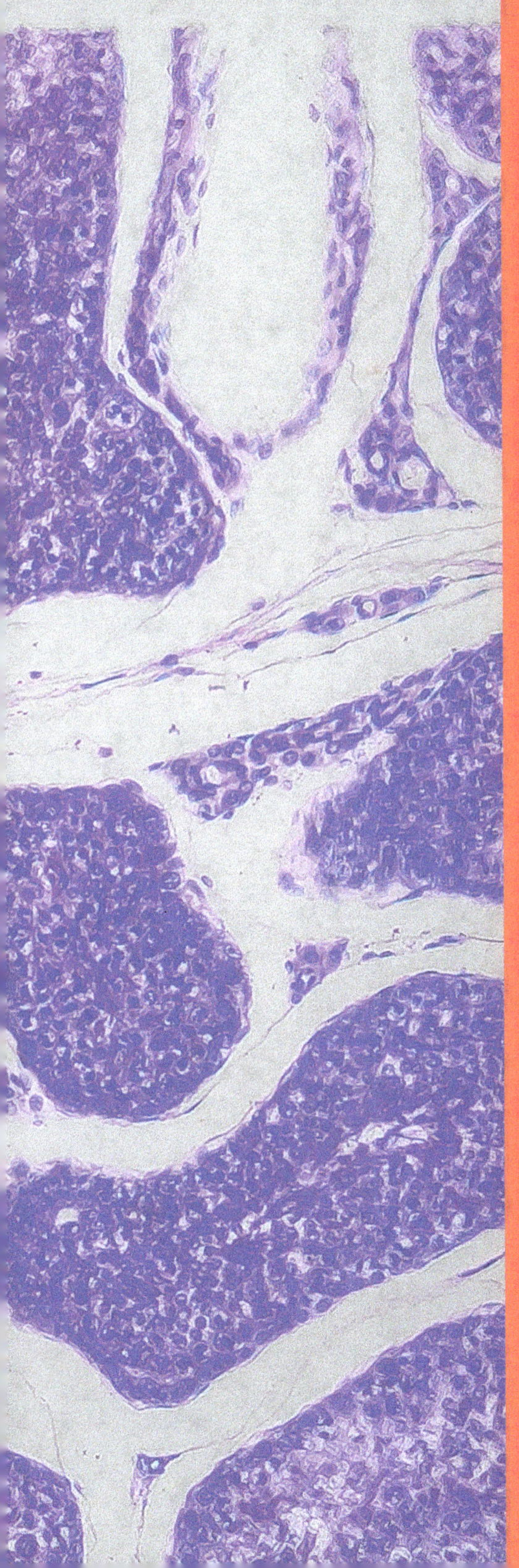

Some animal cells are relatively large while others are very small. However, even the largest of the animal cells can't be seen by the naked eye.

Moreover, an animal cell doesn't have a cell wall. Eukaryotic cells are cells in which the nucleus and organelles are inside the cell membrane. The DNA materials are found in the nucleus.

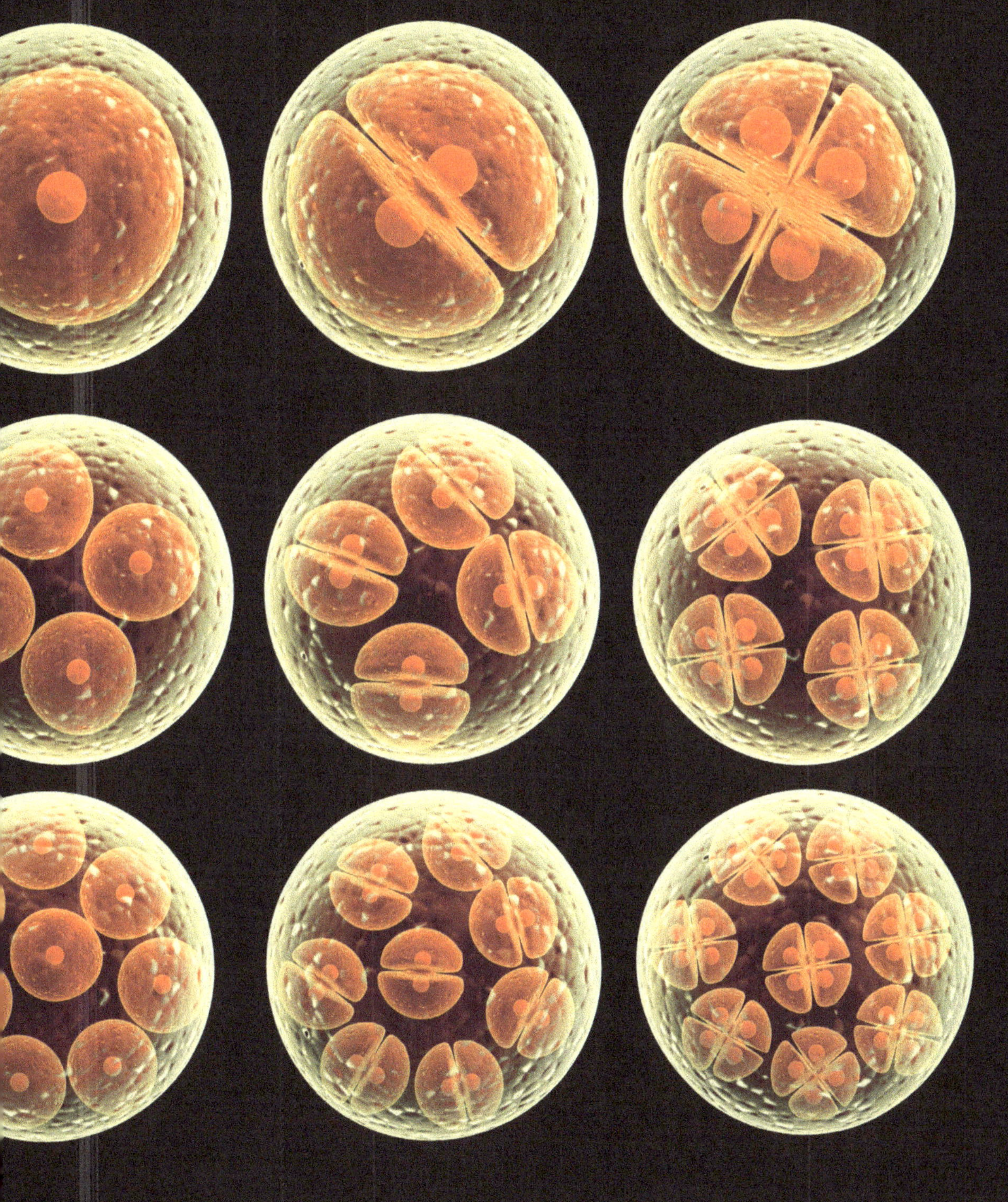

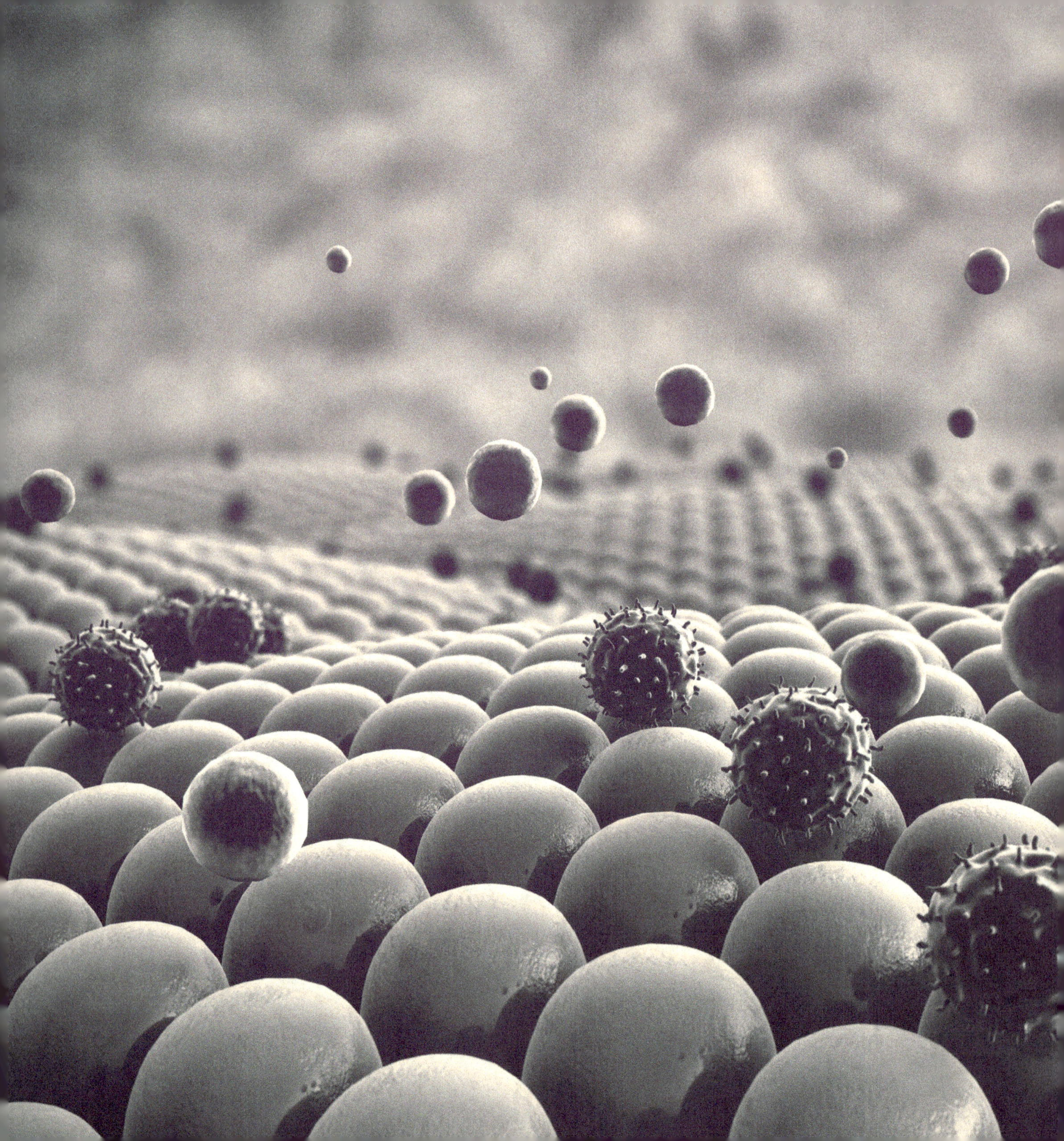

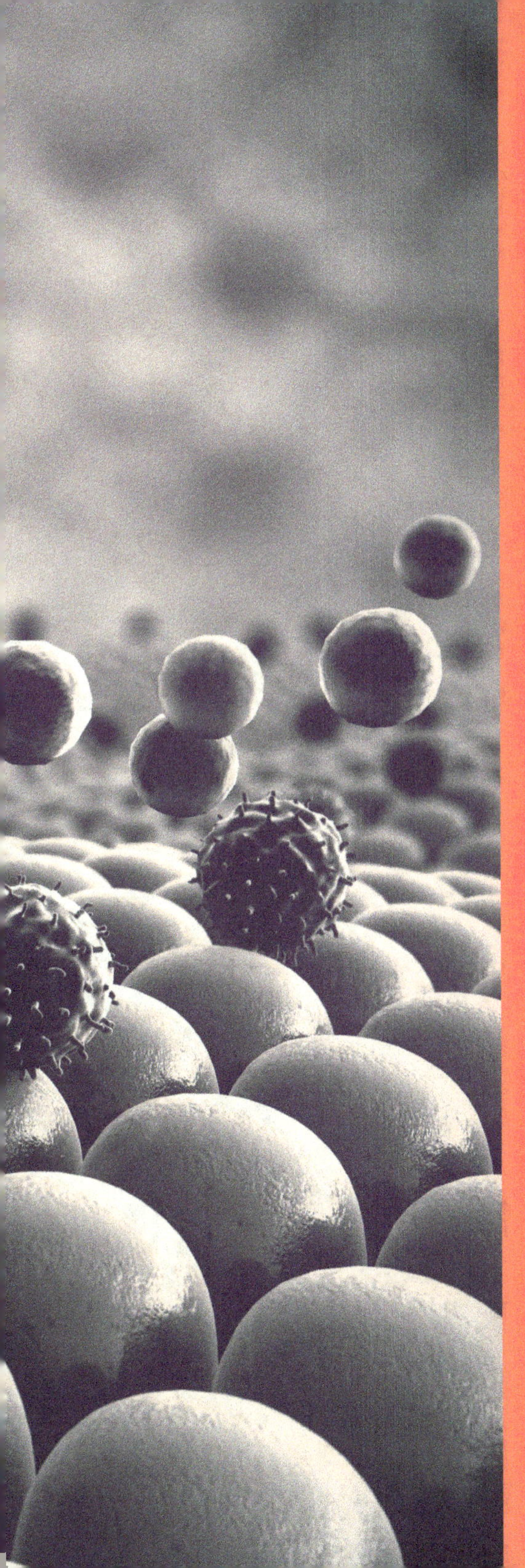

Do you know that animal cells have self-destruction abilities?
This means that they are capable of destroying themselves.

This is done through the process known as Apoptosis or commonly known as "cellular suicide".

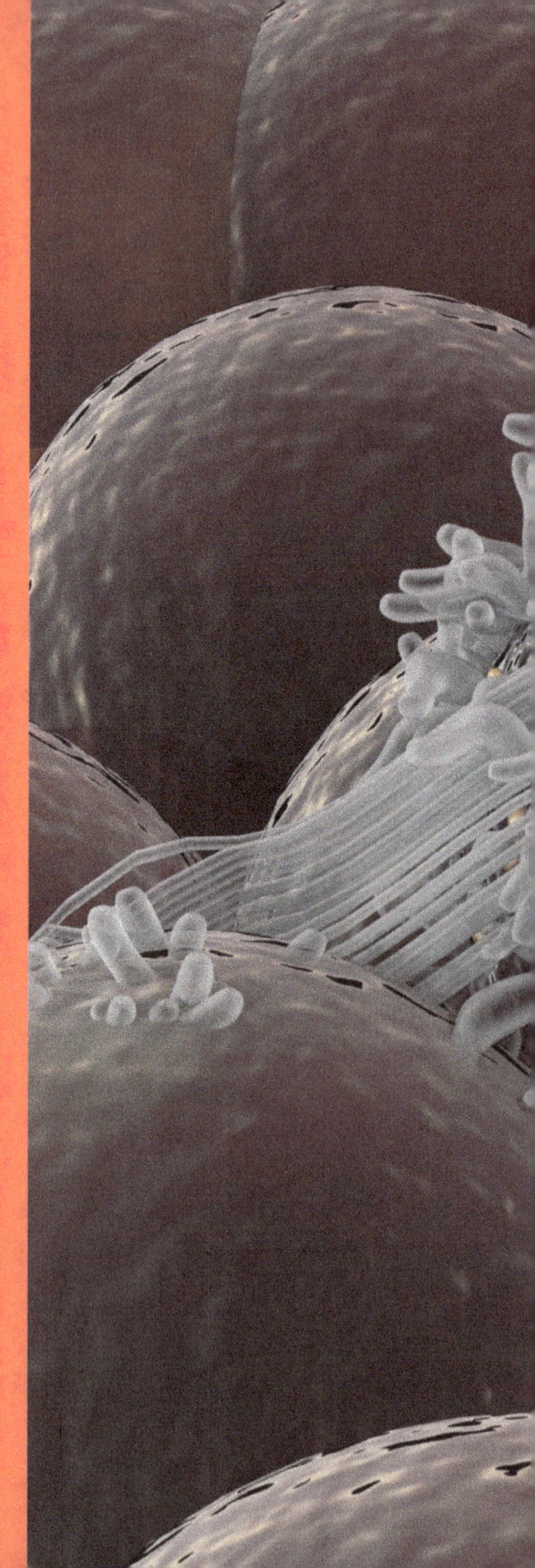

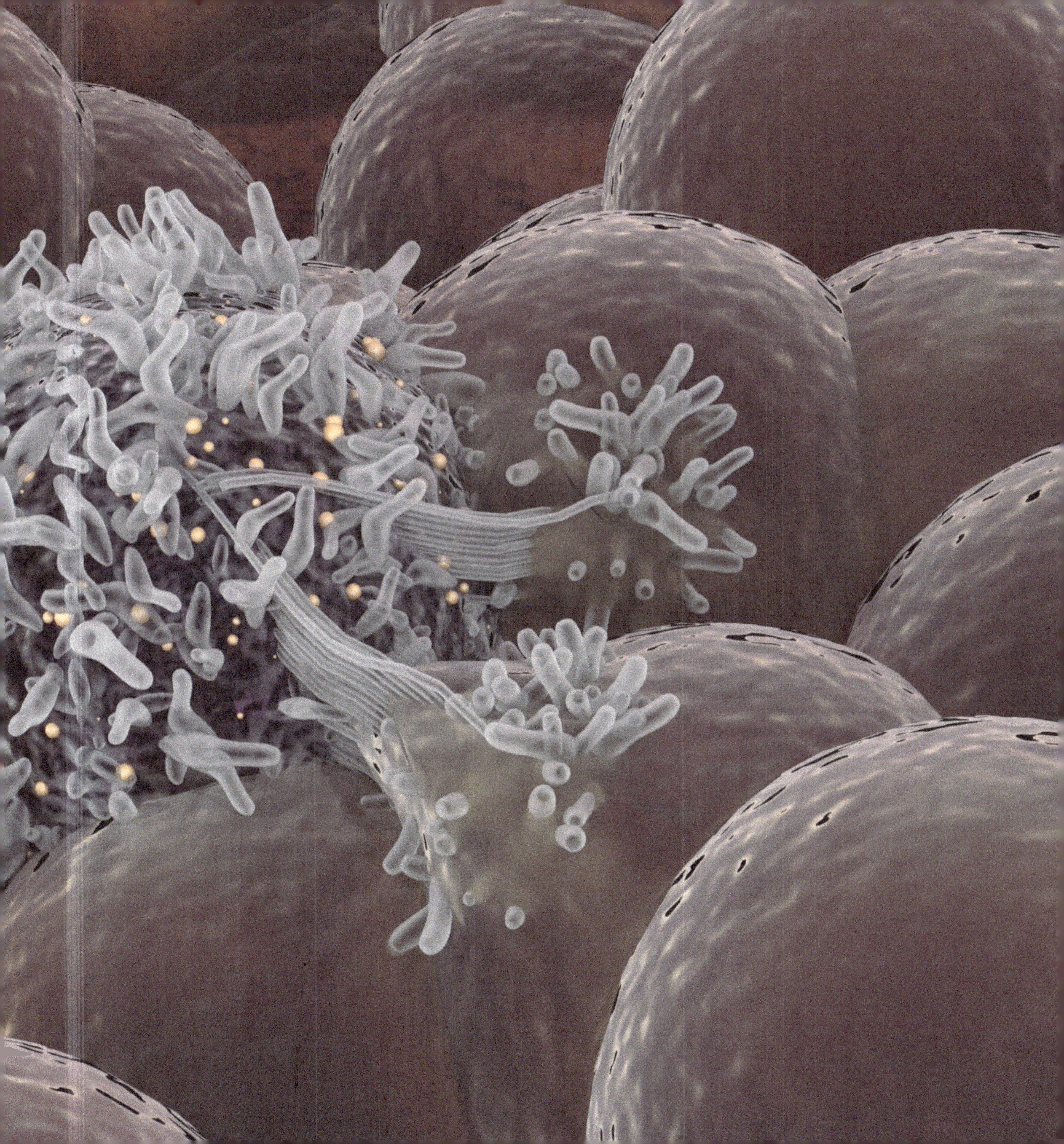

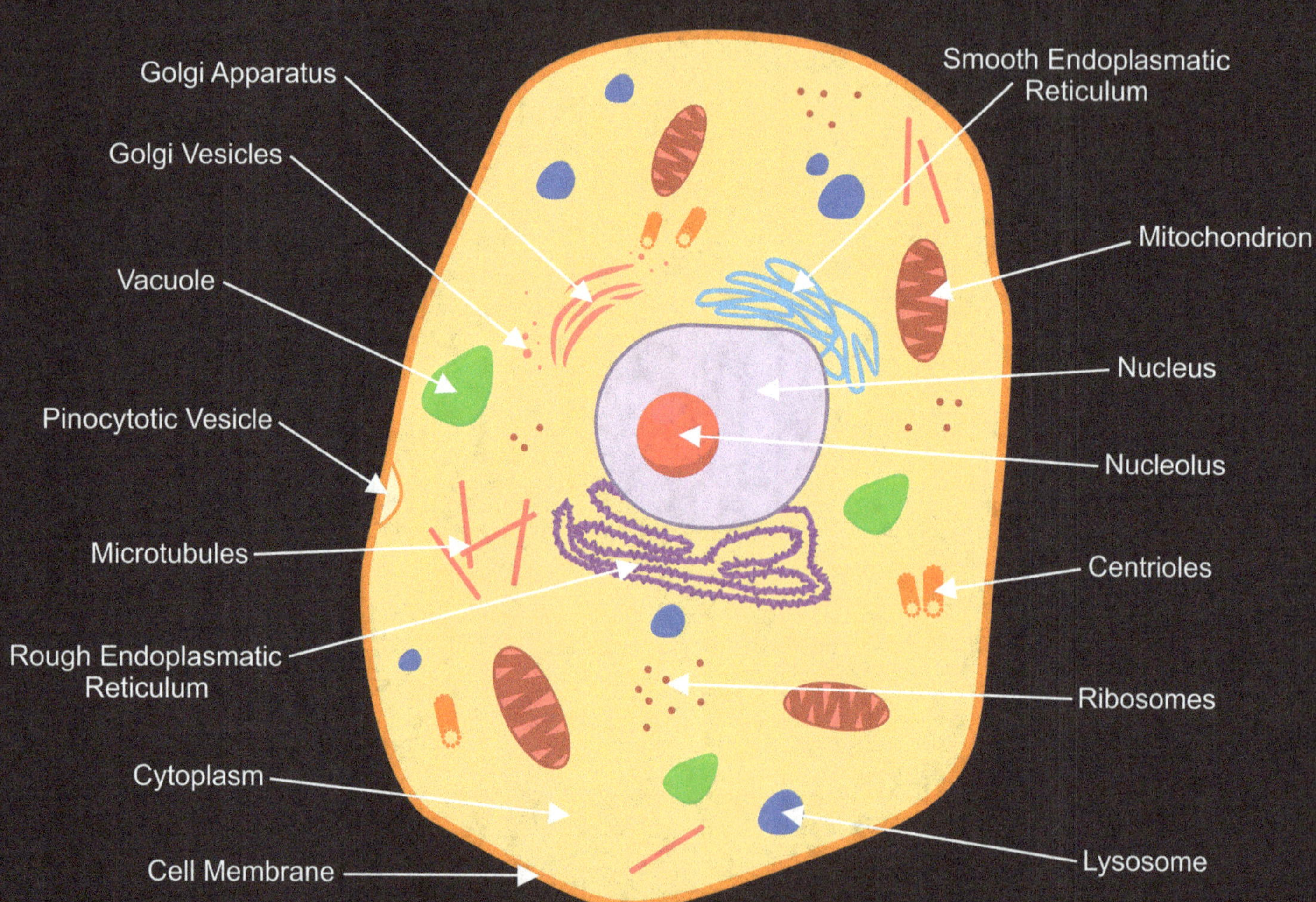

Golgi Apparatus
Golgi Vesicles
Vacuole
Pinocytotic Vesicle
Microtubules
Rough Endoplasmatic Reticulum
Cytoplasm
Cell Membrane
Smooth Endoplasmatic Reticulum
Mitochondrion
Nucleus
Nucleolus
Centrioles
Ribosomes
Lysosome

WHAT ARE ORGANELLES?

Organelles are amazing structures inside the cell which perform different functions. They produce hormones and enzymes. They also provide energy to the cells.

Examples of organelles are centrioles, lysosomes, cilia, and flagella.

An organism is composed of trillions of animal cells.

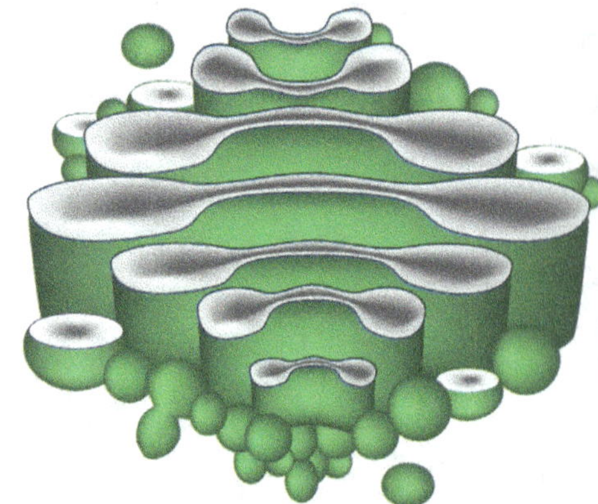

Golgi apparatus

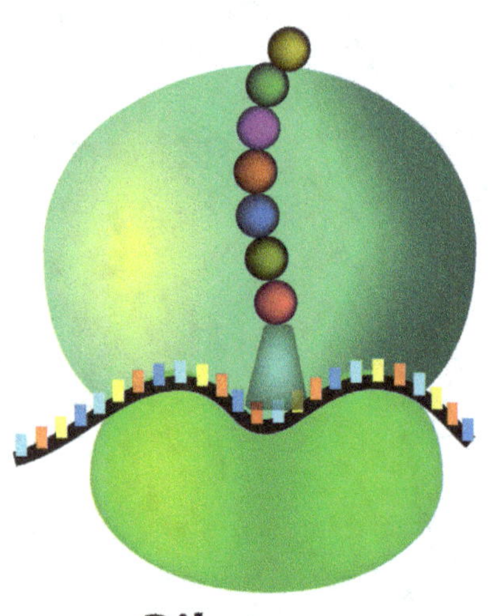

Ribosome

CELL ORGANELLE

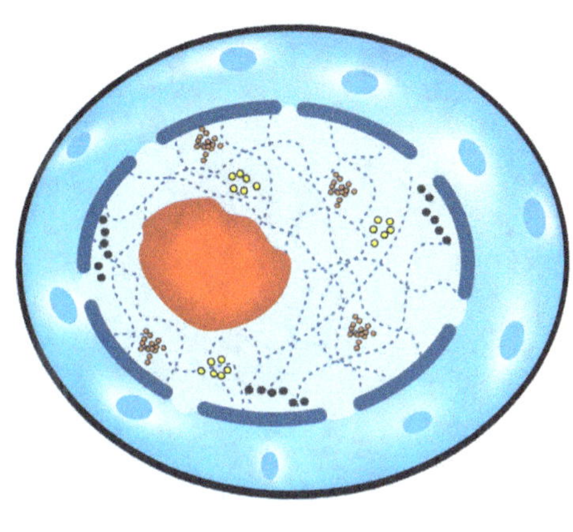

Nucleus

Endoplasmic reticulum

Mitochondrion

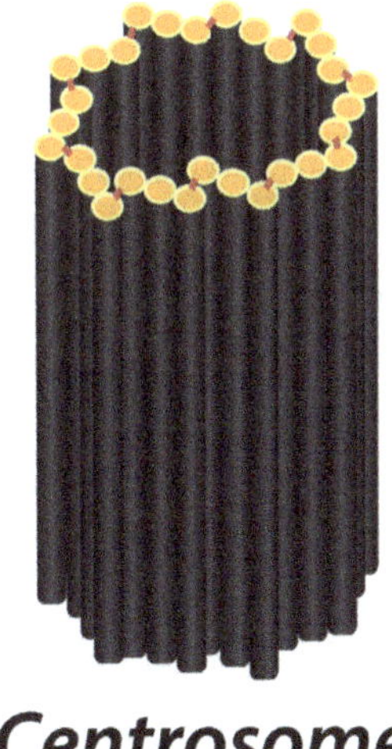

Centrosome

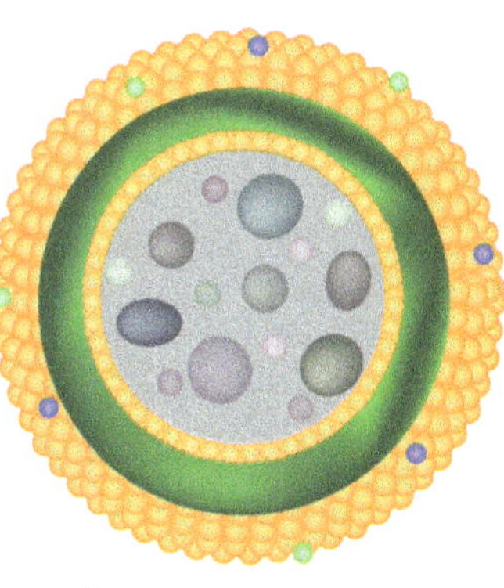

Lysosome

The human body, for example, has many types of animal cells. Each type of cells has amazing biological functions and roles.

REPRODUCTION OF ANIMAL CELLS

Animal cells are reproduced through the process called Mitosis or sexual reproduction. It is the process that involves the ova and the sperm. A new organism is produced when the ova and the sperm meet together in a sexual activity.

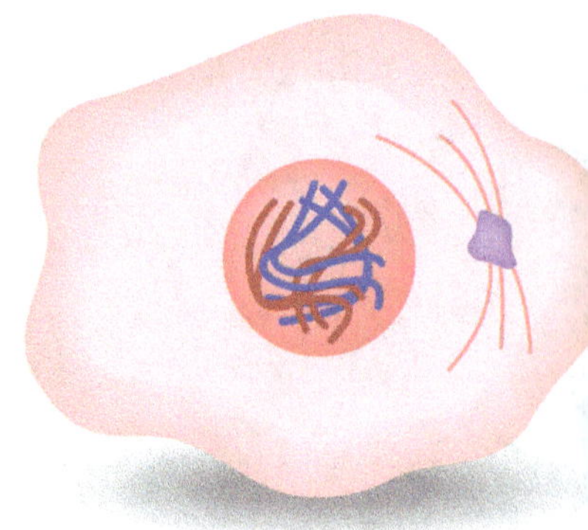

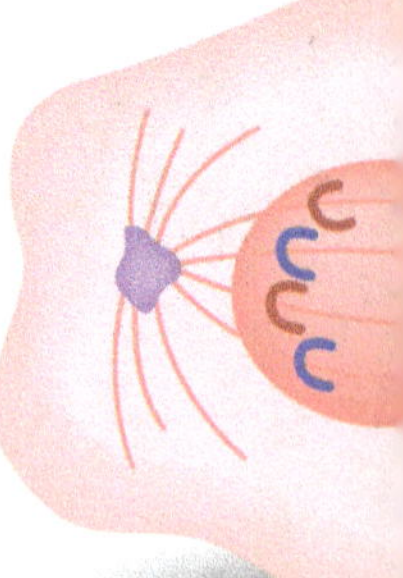

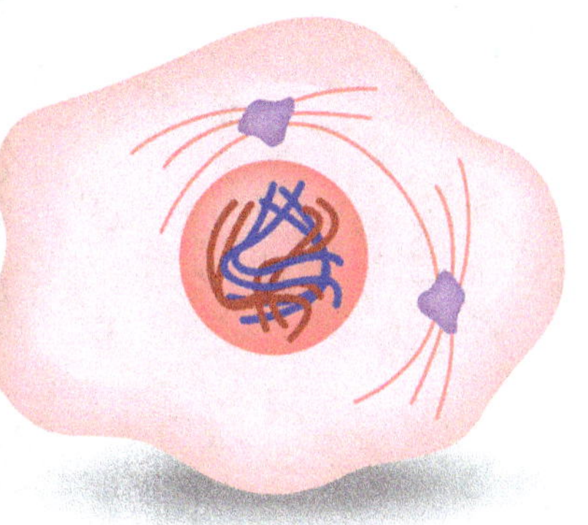

PROPHASE

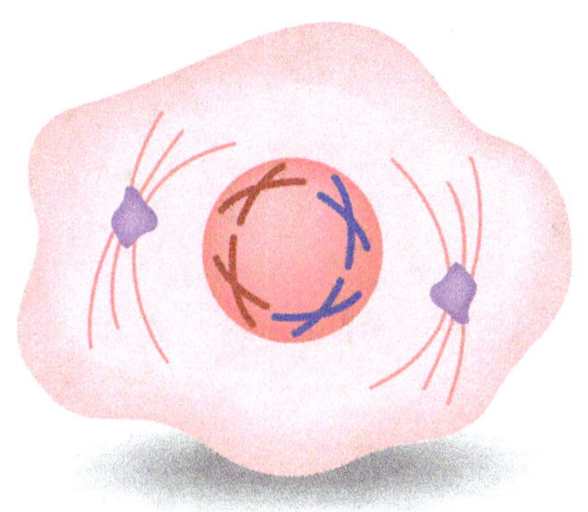

PROMETAPHASE

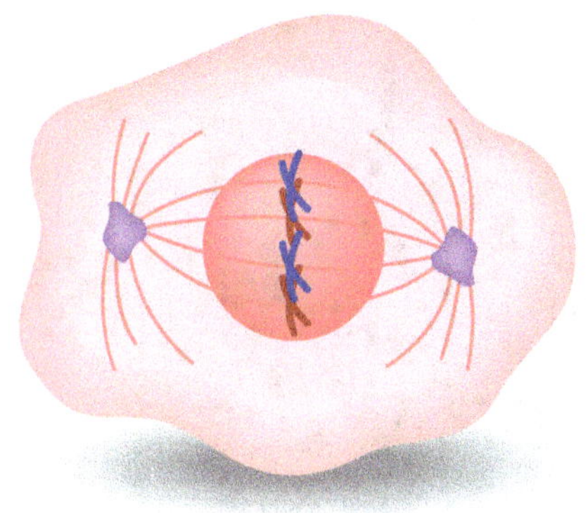

METAPHASE

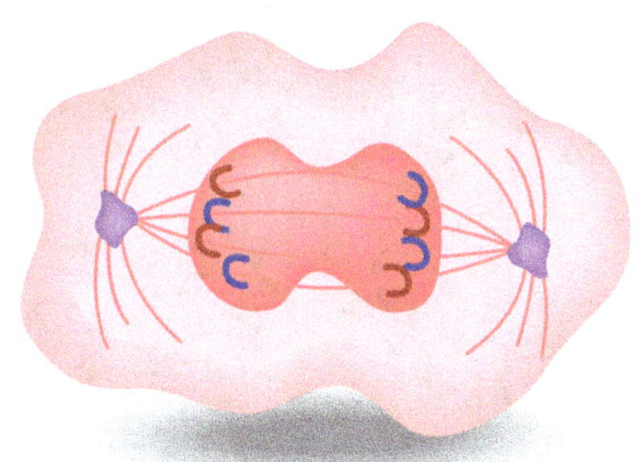

TELOPHASE

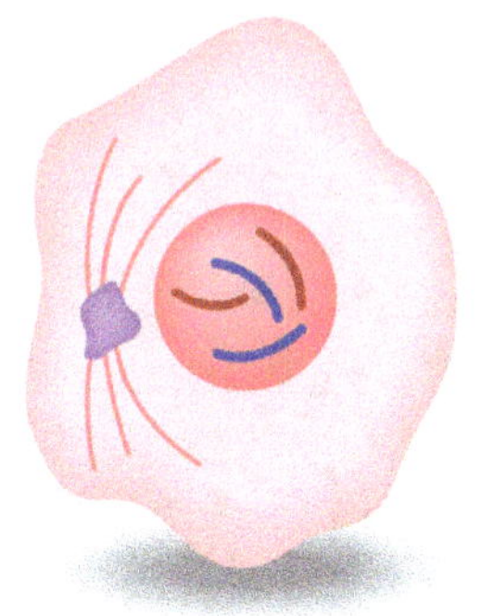

MITOSIS COMPLETED

Did you know that an animal cell is an amazing storehouse? It is because an animal cell comprises all the information and genetic material. These things are needed to make the new organism grow.

In other words, a single animal cell contains the information about biological make-up of an organism including all the traits of an organism.

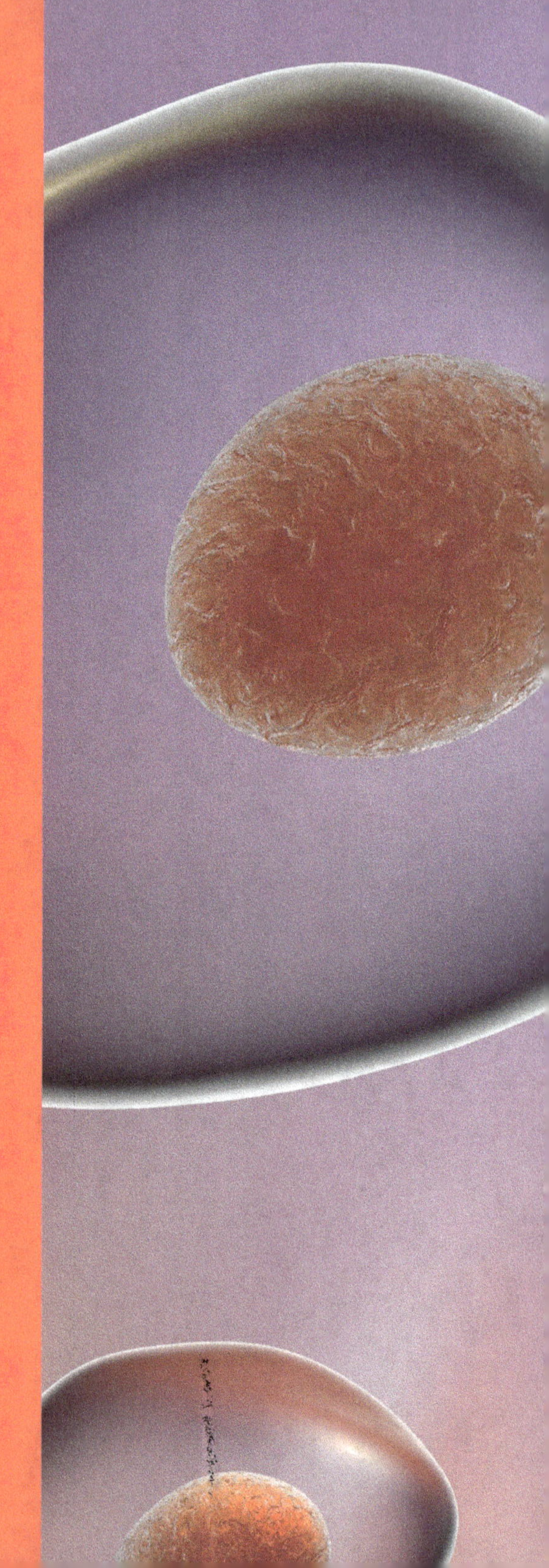

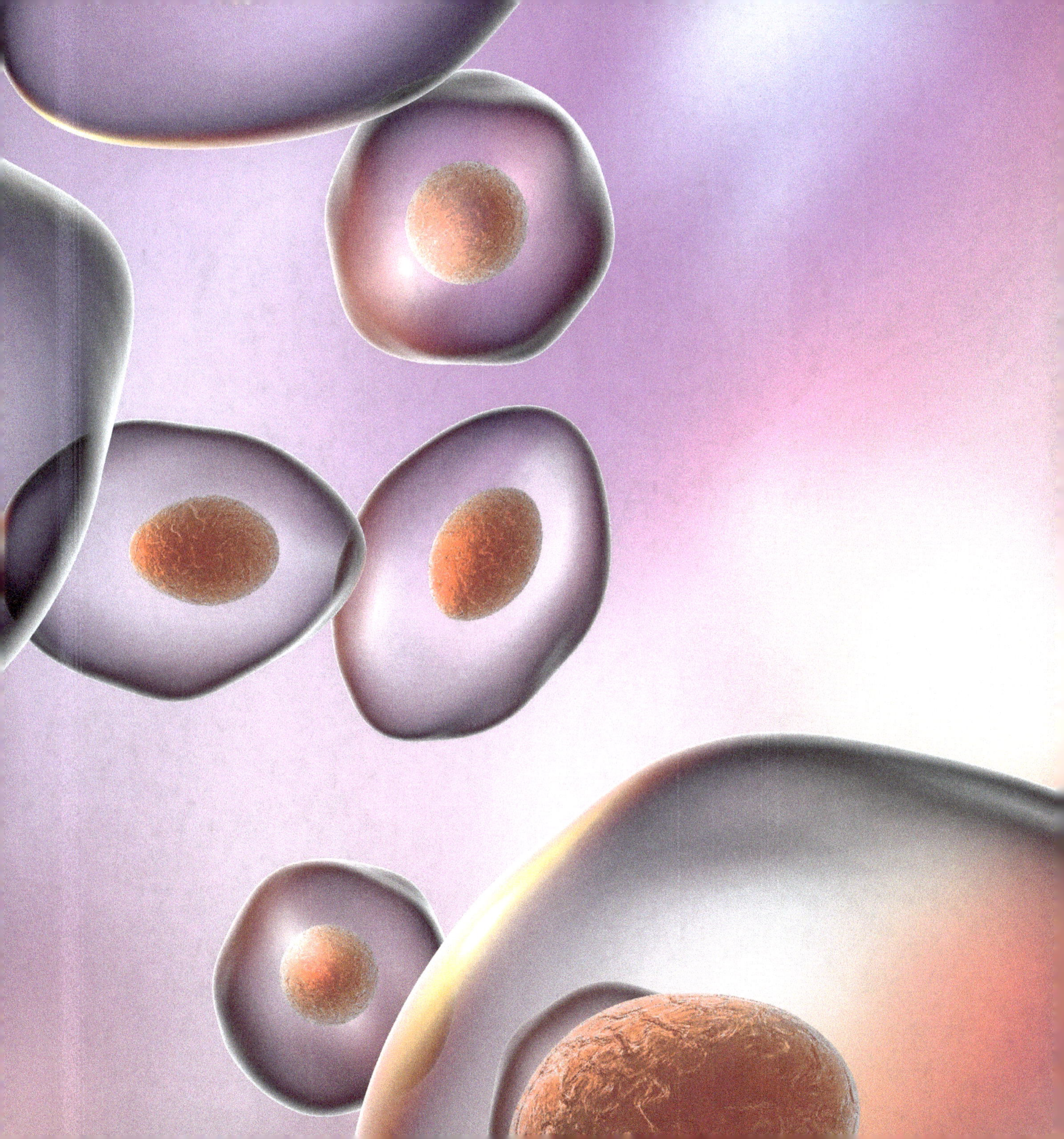

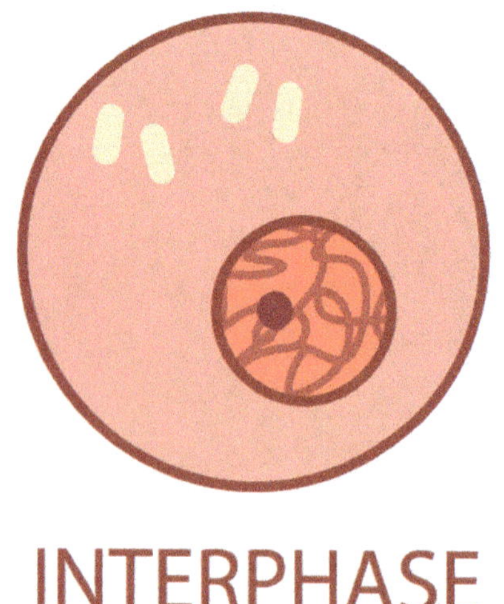

INTERPHASE

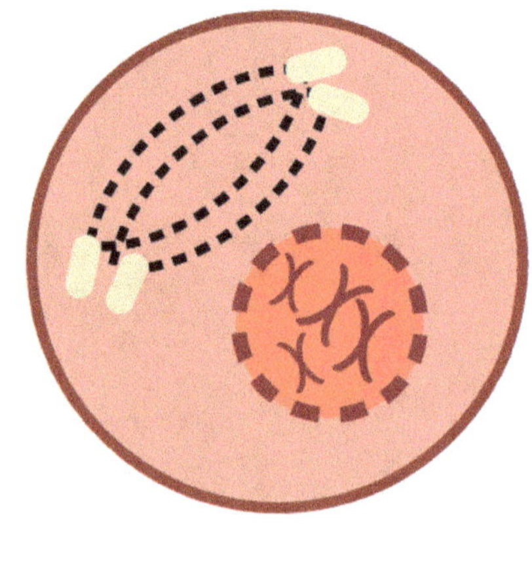

PROPHASE

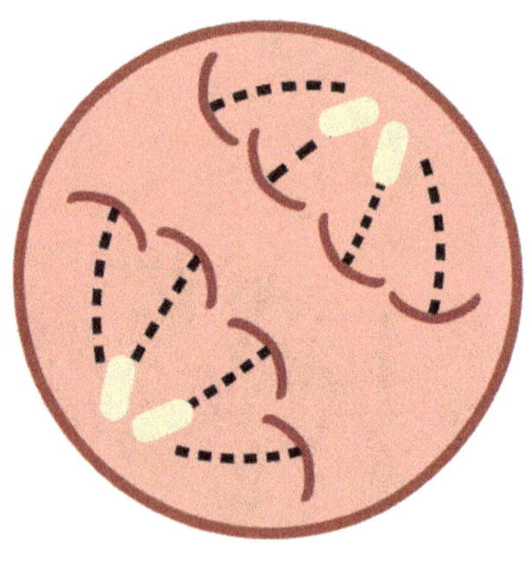

ANAPHASE

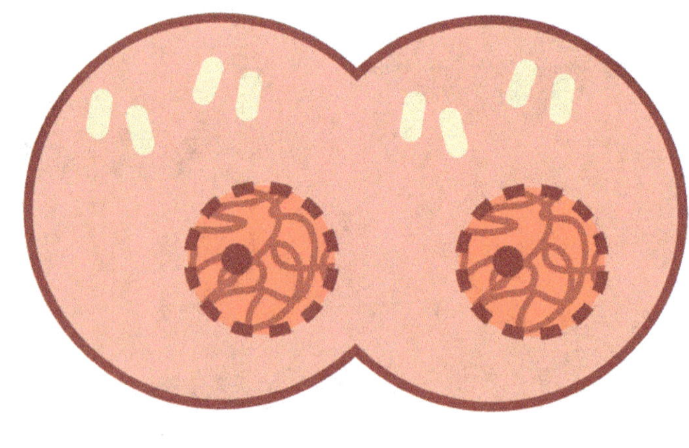

TELOPHASE

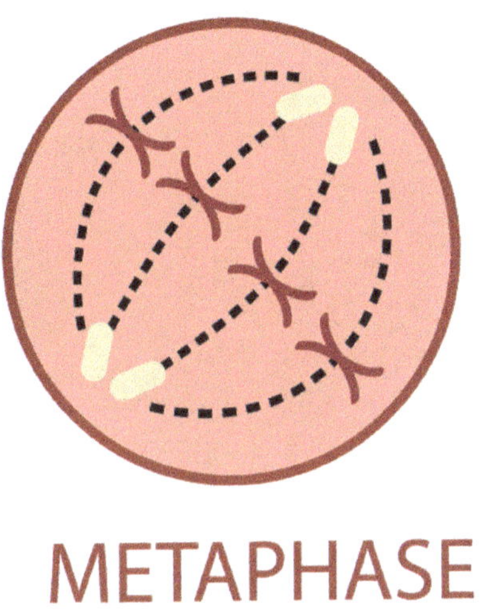

METAPHASE

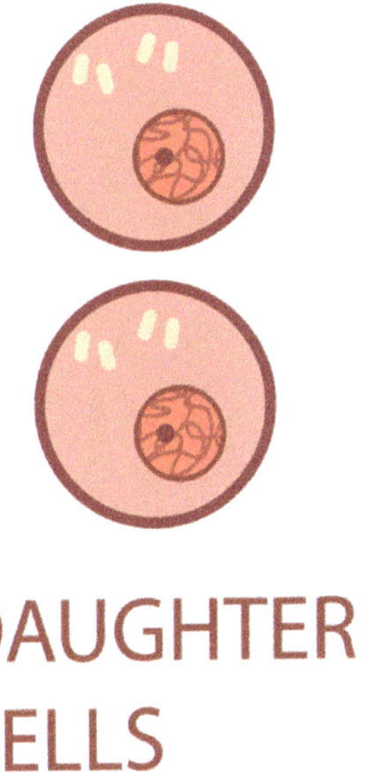

DAUGHTER
CELLS

It is believed that every organism undergoes cell division. Every multi-cellular organism all begin as a fertilized egg.

Eukaryotic cells go through two different types of cell division. In other words, plants, animals, and fungi cells are capable of cell division. These are Meiosis and Mitosis. These are quick yet very complex processes.

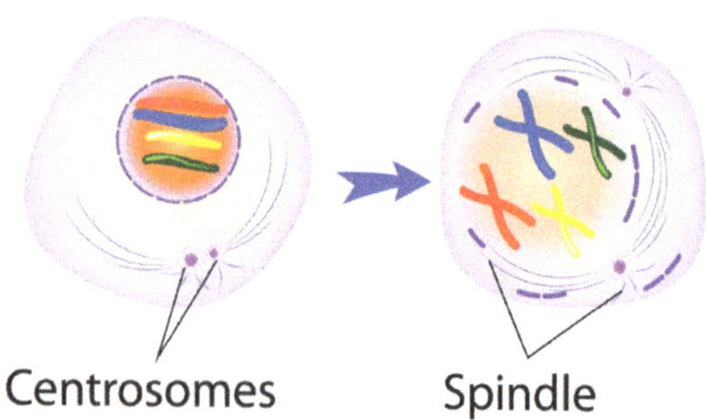

Cell division (meiosis)

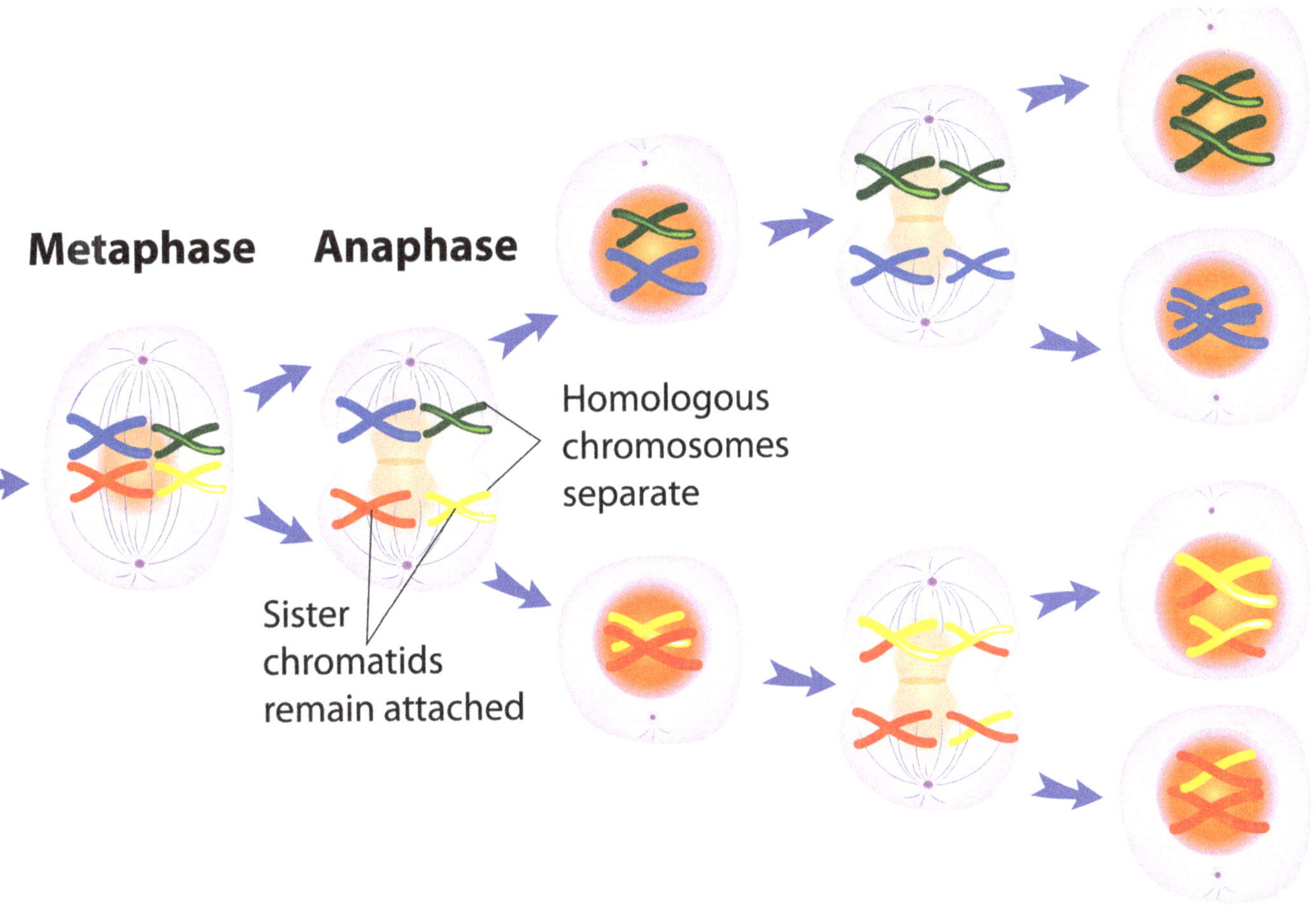

Cell division (mitosis)

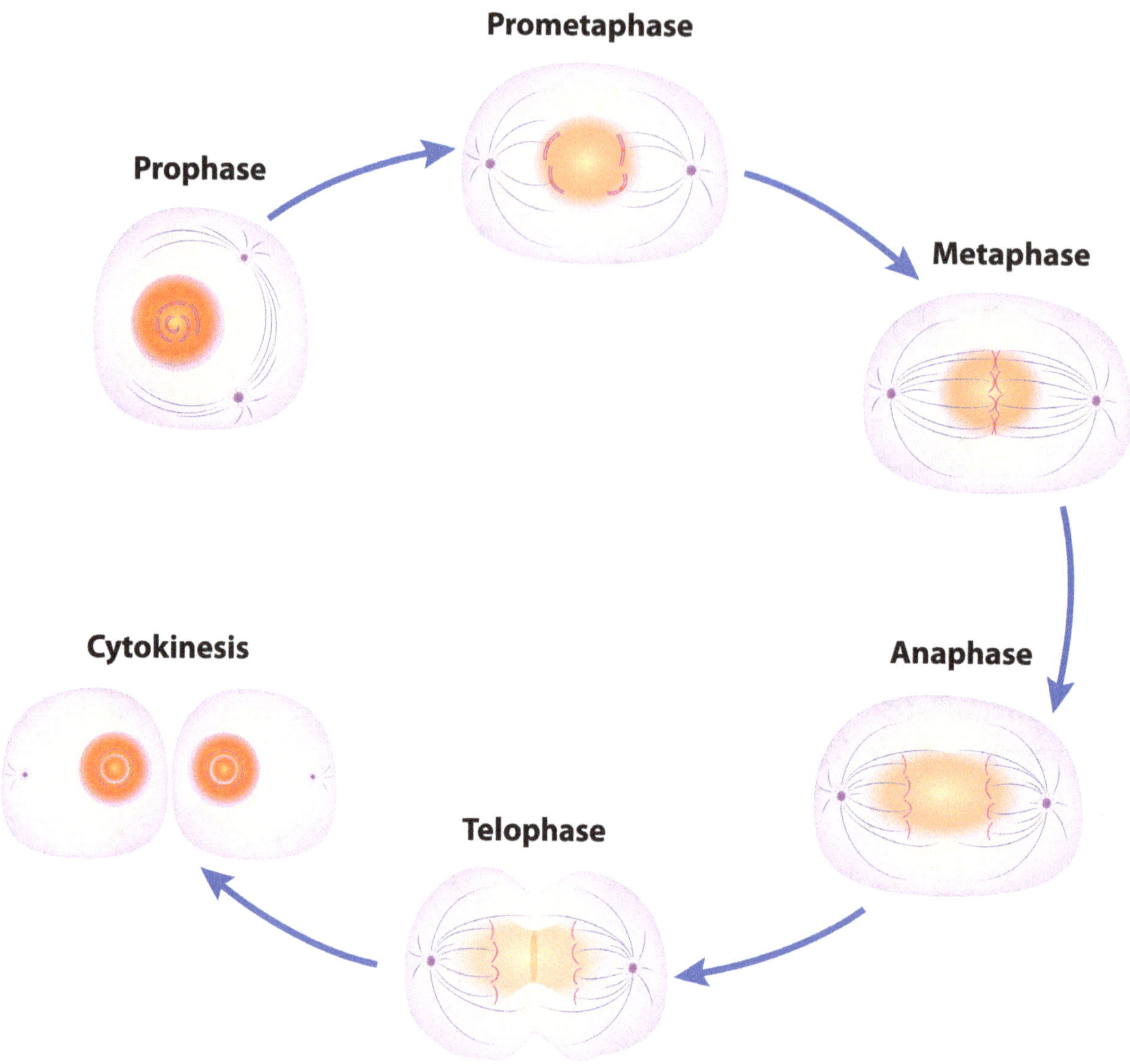

WHAT IS MITOSIS?

It is a type of cell division in which the chromosomes are duplicated. It means an identical copy of them. The chromosomes are scattered equally to the daughter cells.

This equal distribution is known as **Equational division**. Mitosis is divided into five stages. These are the **prophase, prometaphase, metaphase, anaphase, and telophase**.

meiosis

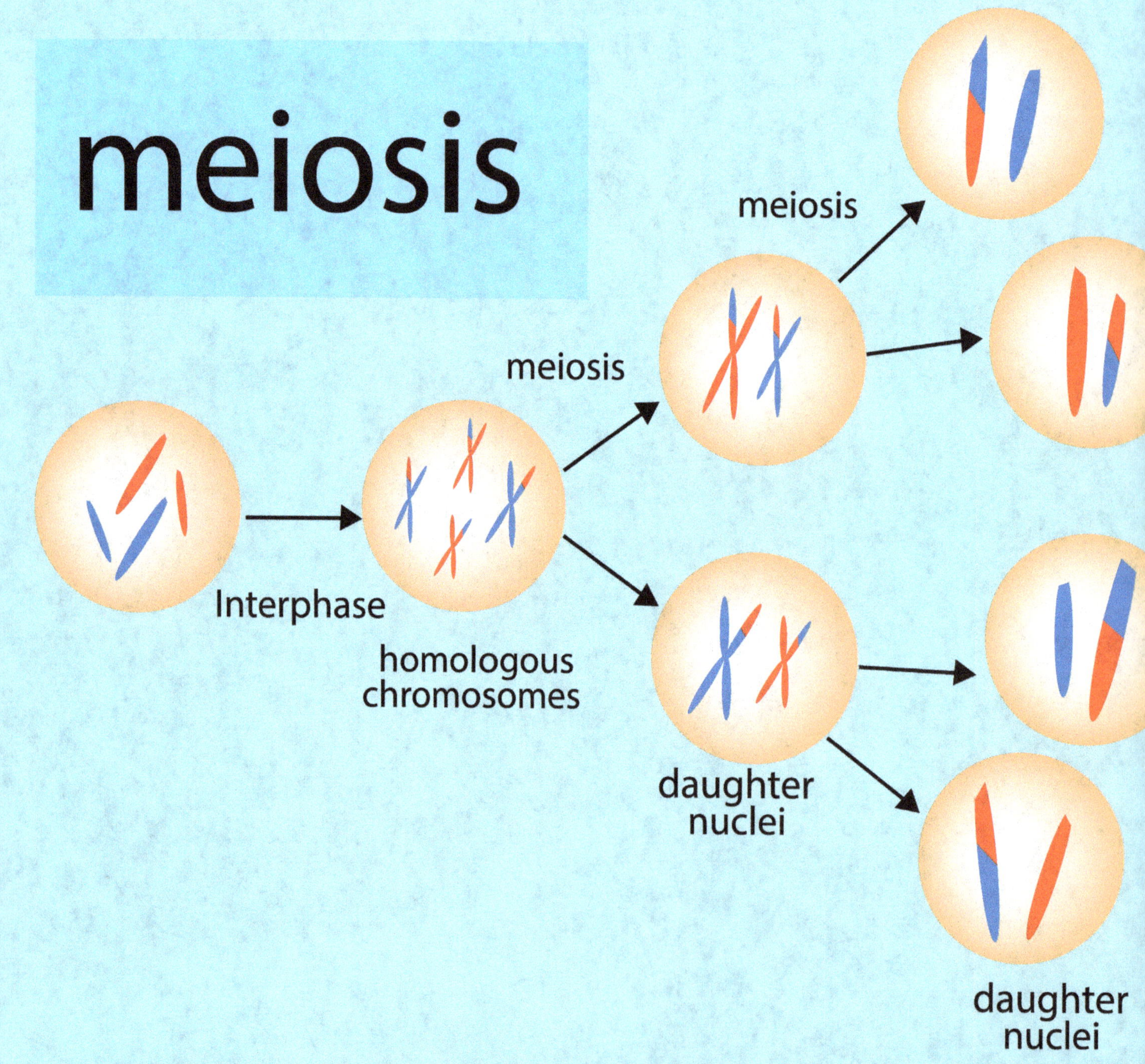

WHAT IS MEIOSIS?

Meiosis is a specialized cell division in which chromosomes are copied and paired up. The paired chromosomes are then separated to create eggs or sperm through sexual reproduction.

It is a process in which the unique genetic information of two parents is combined. It produces reproductive cells. Examples are egg cells, sperm cells, and spores for plants and fungi.

Every living organism on Earth contains amazing structures which originate exactly from a single cell. It just shows how mysterious life is.

Visit

BABY PROFESSOR
EDUCATION KIDS

www.BabyProfessorBooks.com
to download Free Baby Professor eBooks
and view our catalog of new and exciting
Children's Books